I Am Pusheen the Cat

Claire Belton

A Touchstone Book

Published by Simon & Schuster

New York   London   Toronto   Sydney   New Delhi

Touchstone

An Imprint of Simon & Schuster, Inc.

1230 Avenue of the Americas

New York, NY 10020

First Touchstone trade paperback edition October 2013

TOUCHSTONE and colophon are registered trademarks of Simon & Schuster, Inc.

For information about special discounts for bulk purchases, please contact Simon & Schuster Special Sales at 1-866-506-1949 or business@simonandschuster.com.

The Simon & Schuster Speakers Bureau can bring authors to your live event. For more information or to book an event, contact the Simon & Schuster Speakers Bureau at 1-866-248-3049 or visit our website at www.simonspeakers.com.

Interior design by Joy O'Meara

Manufactured in the United States of America

19 20

Library of Congress Cataloging-in-Publication data is available.

ISBN 978-1-4767-4701-9
ISBN 978-1-4767-4712-5 (ebook)

For Sarah and Jake.

Special thanks to Kathleen Belton for her help
preparing the illustrations for print.

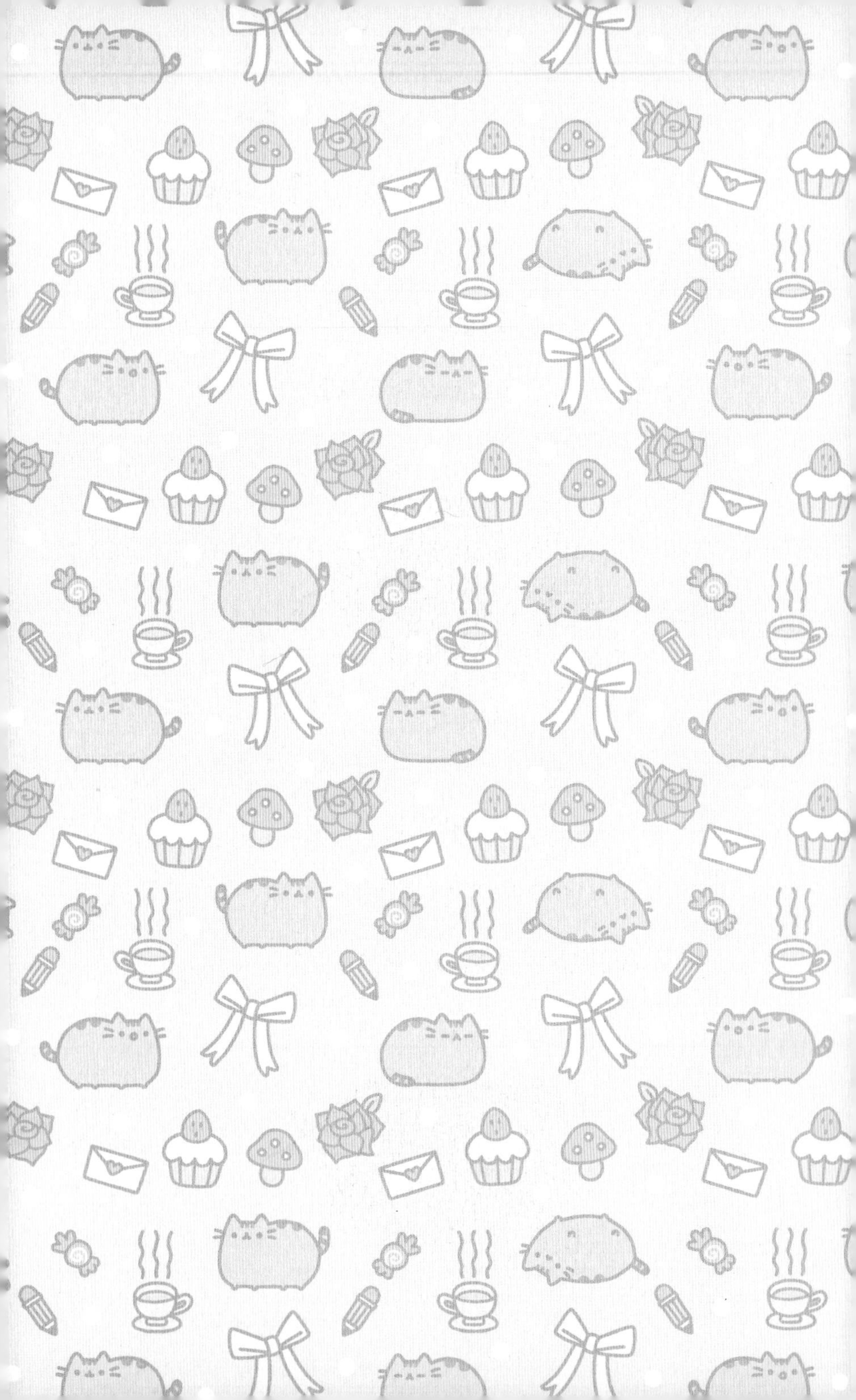

Contents

Part I

I Am Pusheen the Cat

1

Part II

Things You Should
Know About Cats

33

Contents

Part III

How to Live

65

Part IV

Stormy

101

Contents

Part V

A Year in the Life of Pusheen

121

Acknowledgments

175

Part I

I Am Pusheen the Cat

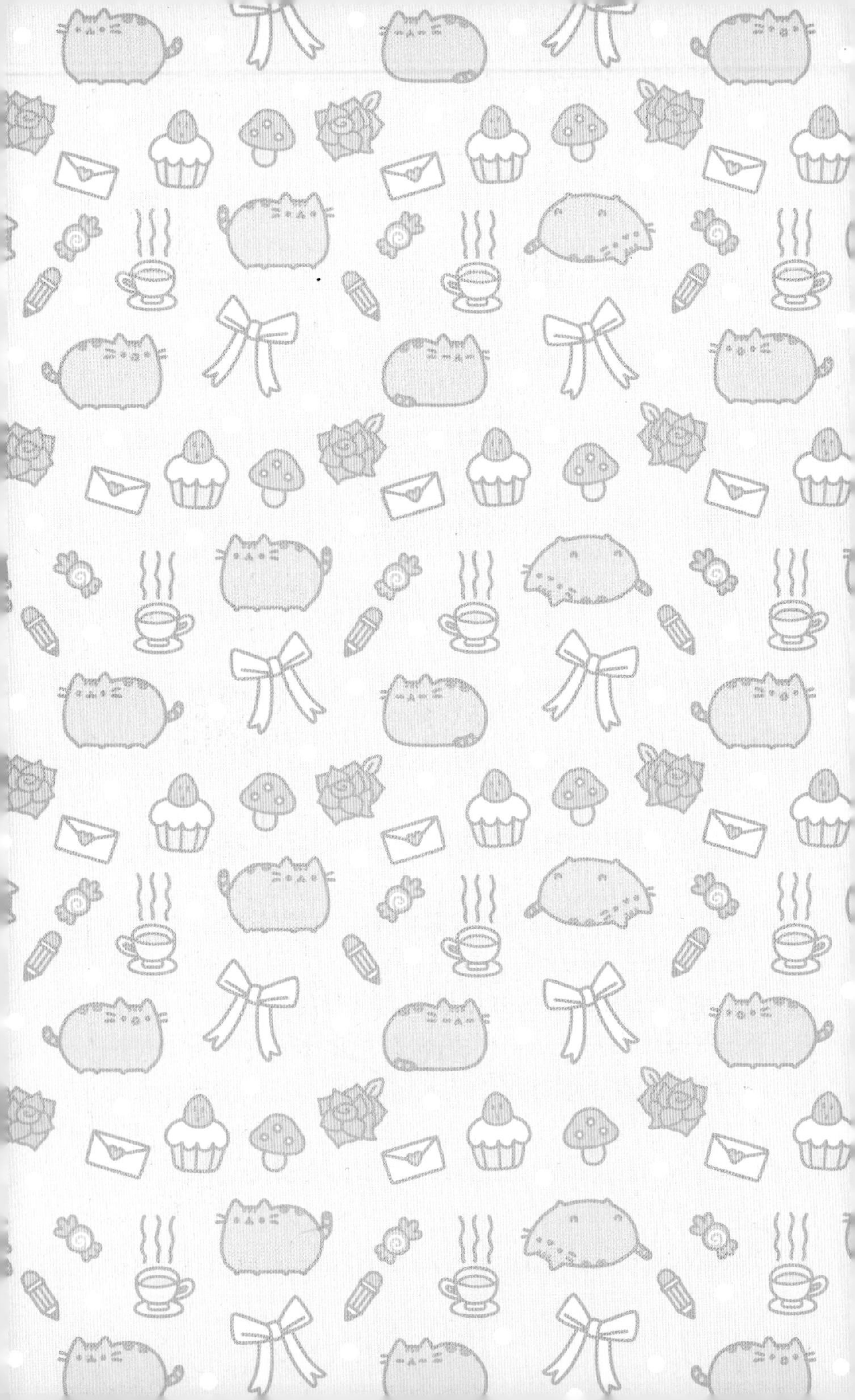

Name: Pusheen
Birthday: Feb 18
Sex: Female
Best feature: My toe beans
Where I live: In the house
Hobbies: Blogging, sleeping
Favorite food: All of them
Favorite word: "Meow"
Dream: To make friends all over the world

♥ Things that I love ♥

Music

Food

Friends

Family

Sleep

Internet

Petting chart

- ☐ Yes, please!
- ☐ Okay.
- ☐ I will bite you.

My perfect weekend

Eat everything

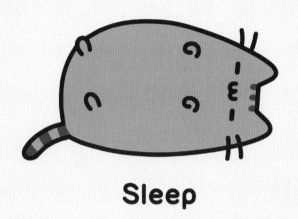

Sleep

Chill with friends

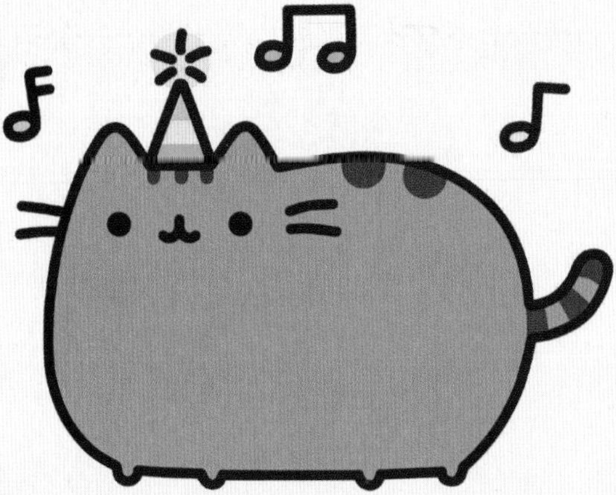

Party

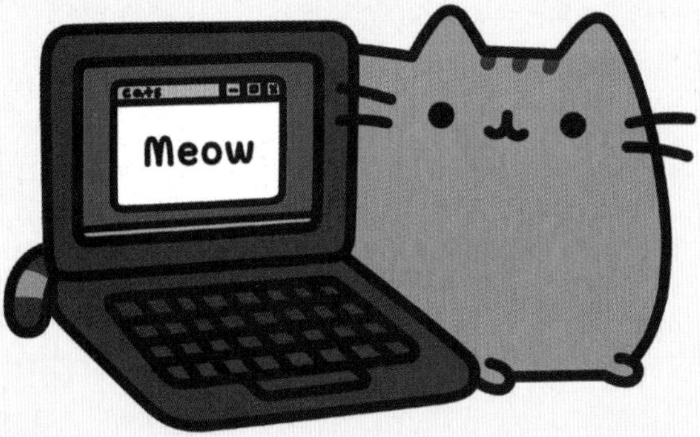
Meow

Blog

My weekend plans:

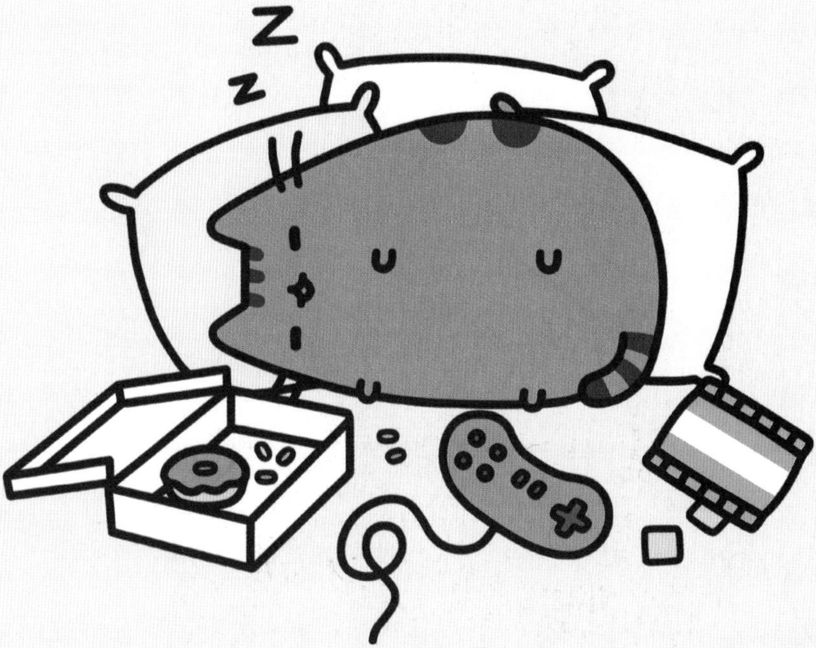
Z
z

Pusheen's guide to "acquiring" treats

1. Case the joint

2. Consume the target

3. Destroy the evidence

4. No remorse

Pusheen's guide to being friendly

Not friendly

Kind of friendly?

Friendly

Too friendly

Pusheen's guide to sleeping positions

The beached whale

The roast turkey

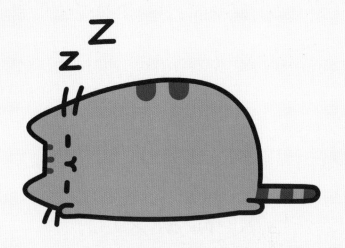

The superhero

The horizontal zombie

If I were tiny, I would...

get groomed with a toothbrush

play with thread

bathe in a teacup

sleep on a marshmallow

If cats were giant

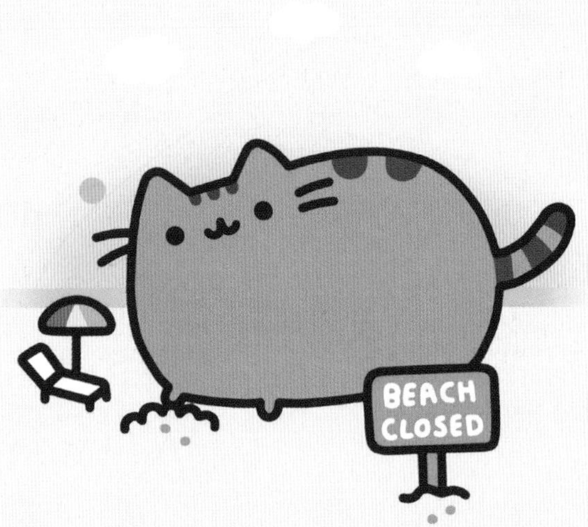
BEACH
CLOSED

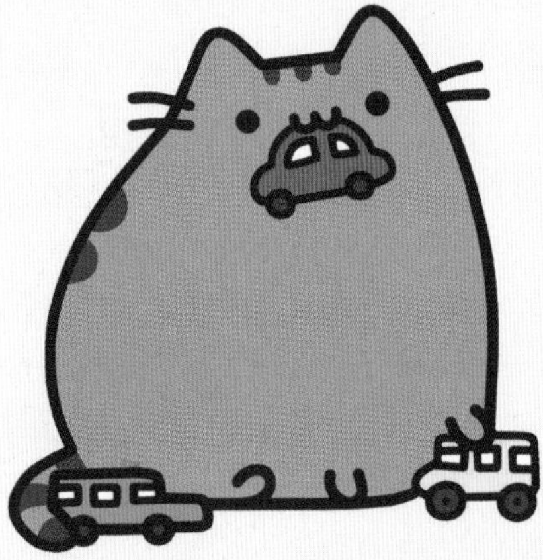

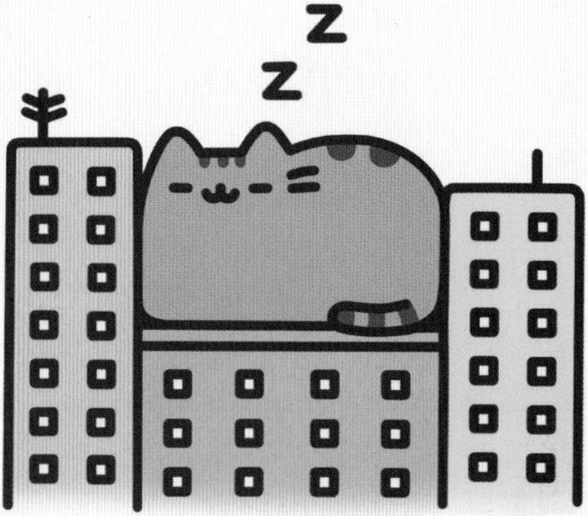
Z
Z

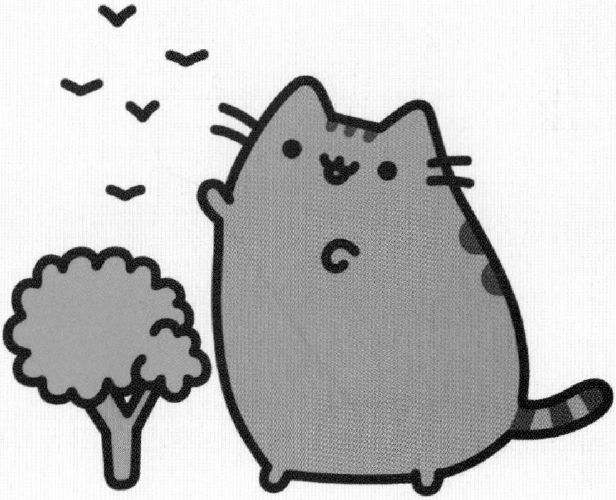

Pusheen's guide to
being lazy

Kind of lazy

Lazy

Very lazy

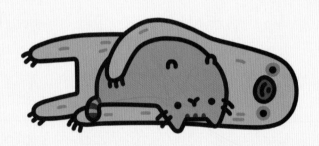

Super lazy

So lazy

can't move

5

Pusheen Games

1. Lick cold things

ice

window

door

2. Sleep inconveniently

on remote

on keyboard

← can't
move

on children

3. Yodeling
(at 2:00 am)

mrowwyrowahhrrrmroww
wahhhrowww mrrowwahhh
rarrmrrwraaamyoooo

4. Contortion

so
yummy

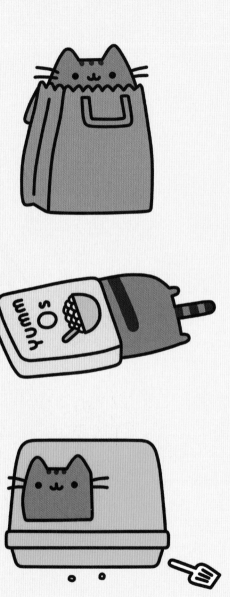

5. 3-meter dash

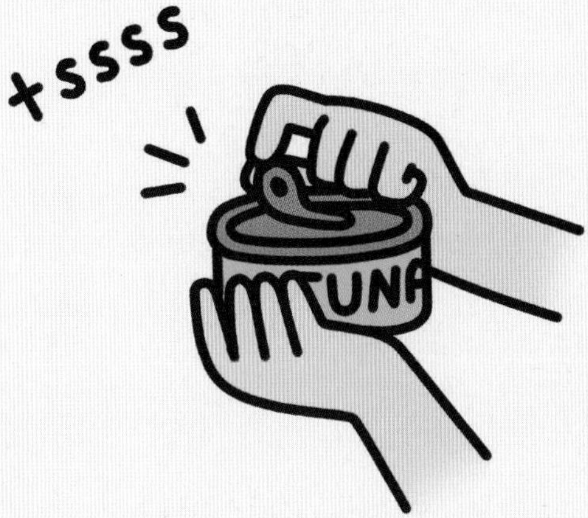
tssss
UNA

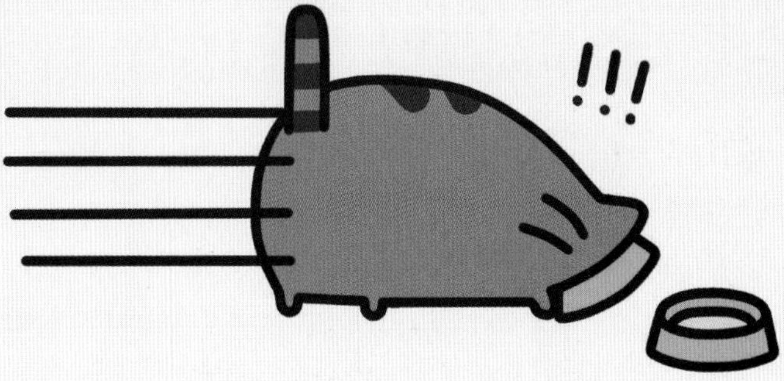
!!!

I like to drink with a straw

and pretend I'm a tiny elephant

I love snuggles

Part II

Things You Should Know About Cats

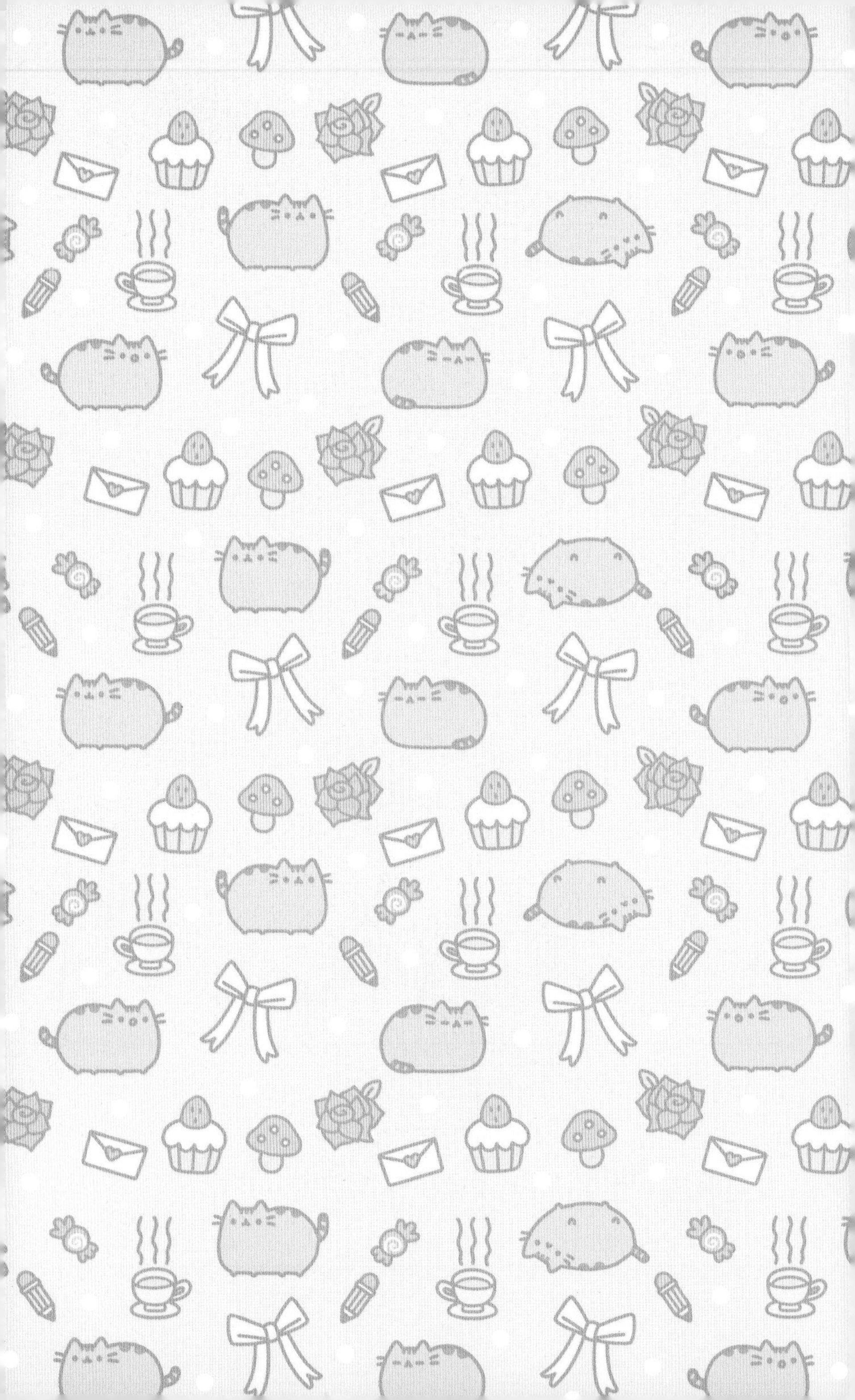

Understanding your cat's
emotions

Happiness
(I've eaten recently)

Sadness
(I want more food)

Anger
(Give me more food)

Curiosity
(Where is the food?)

Contentment
(I ate all of the food)

Fear
(Will there be more?)

Things that cats kind of look like

Cat

Seal

Cat

Owl

Cat

?????

Career options
for your cat

Baker

Pianist

Masseuse

Sculptor

Blogger

DJ

Things that cats apparently don't mind

Scary stories

for your cat

Once upon a time...

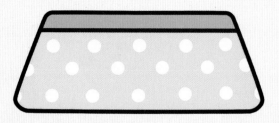

There was a food bowl.

It was empty.

The end.

Once upon a time...

There was a bathtub.

There were cats in it.

The end.

Once upon a time...

There was a vacuum cleaner.

The end.

Cat Etiquette

Remove kibbles from your
dish before eating them.

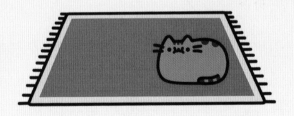

If you must barf,
do so on the rug.

If standing on someone,
face them with your butt.

Only scratch furniture
when you feel like it.

Be sure to kick litter
all over the floor.

Don't forget to shed
on everything!

DinoCats

Felineosaurus Rex

Stareosaurus

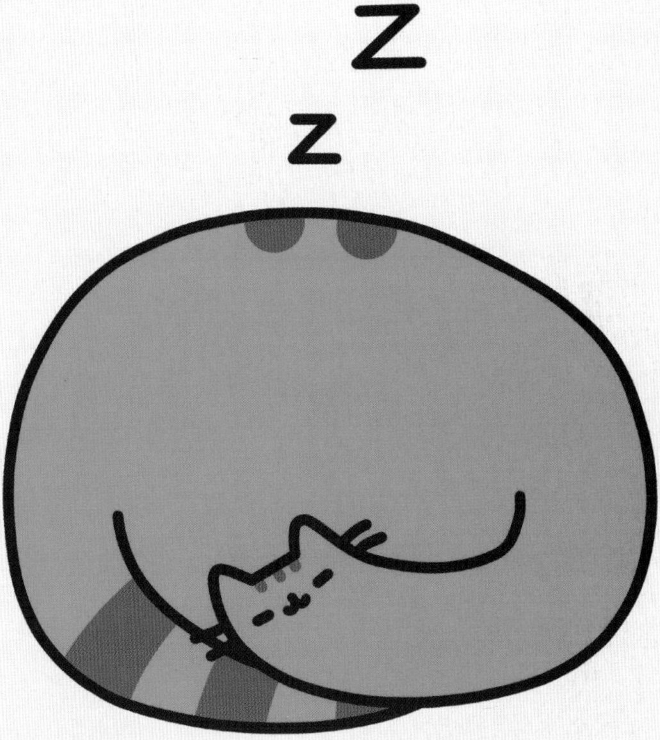
Z
Z

Anaposaurus

Tearodactyl

Velocicator

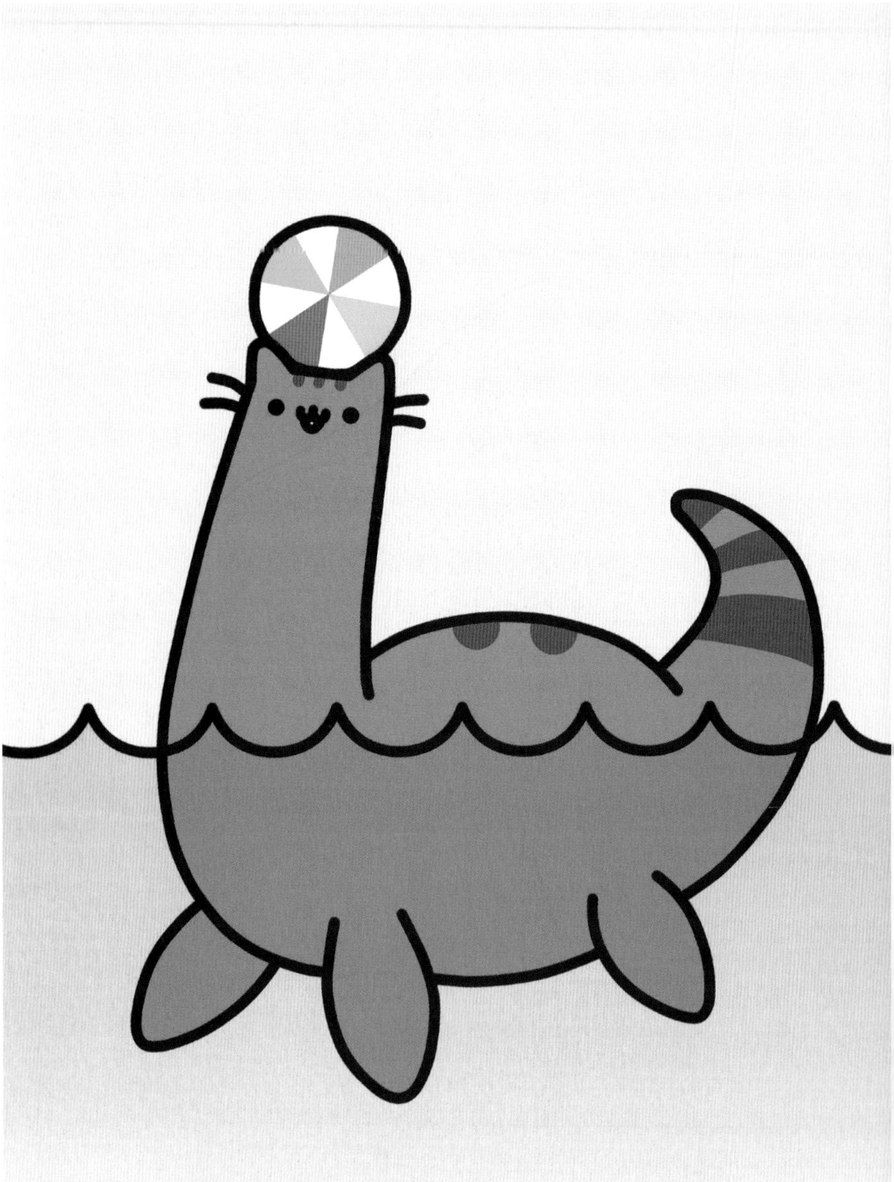

Playsosaurus

6 reasons you should consider being a cat

1. Free food

2. Free rent

3. Sleep as long as you want to

4. Look great with no effort

5. Toes look like beans

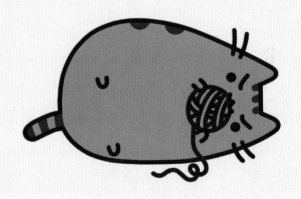

6. License to *kill*

Places that cats belong

The sink: No

Your shoes: No

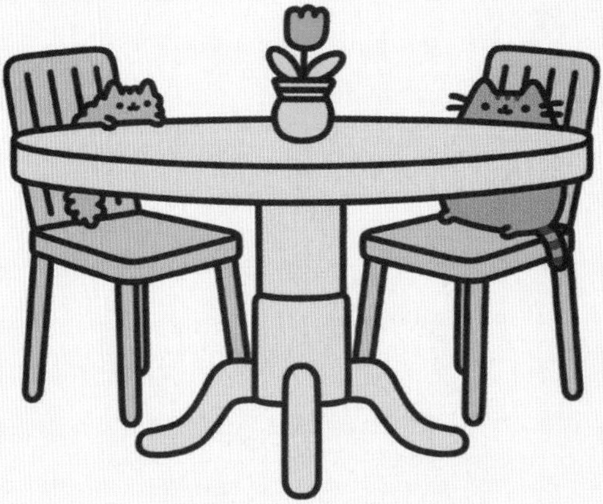

The table: No

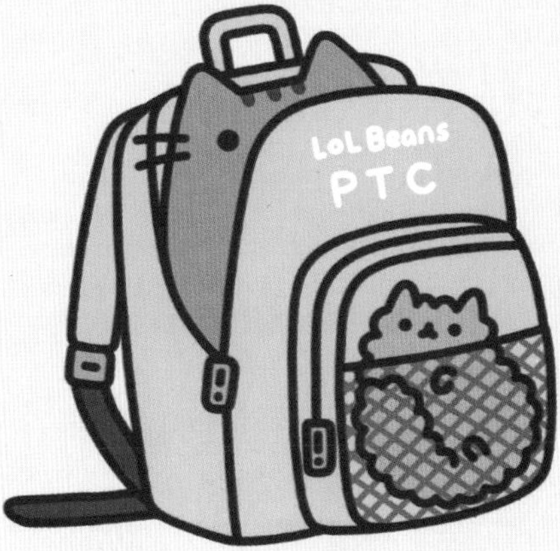
LoL Beans
PTC

Your bag: No

This thing: ???

Your heart: Yes

Part III

How to Live

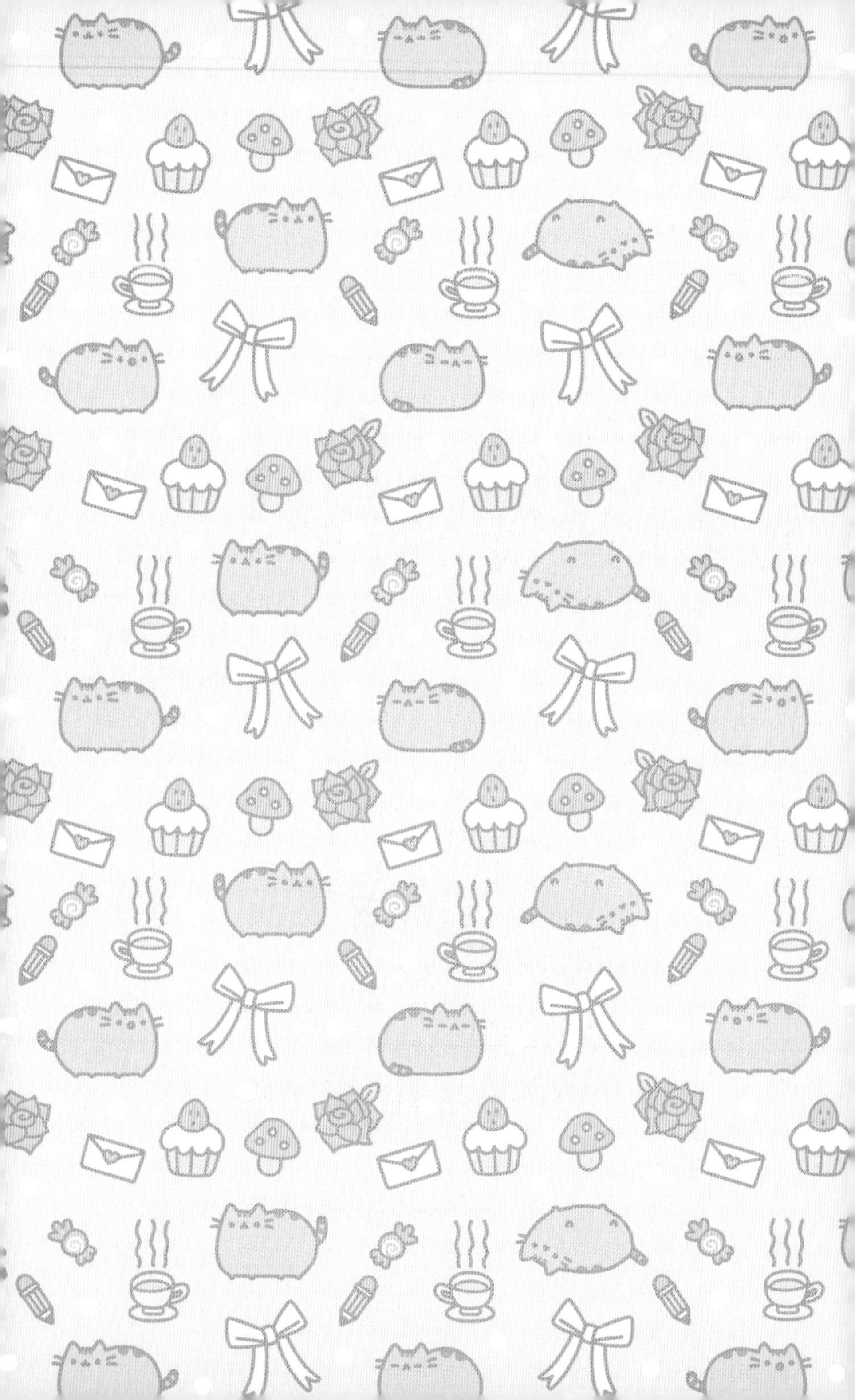

6 practical uses for
Marshmallows

1. Slippers

2. Earplugs

3. A nice hat

4. A tiny chair

5. A cool toy

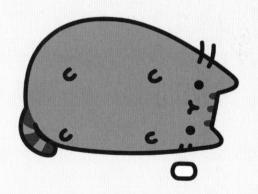

6. A role model

How to tie a tie

The best places to sleep

No

Yes

No

Yes

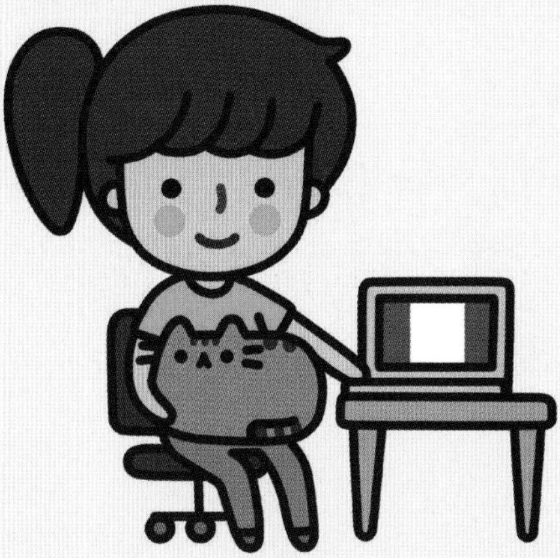

No

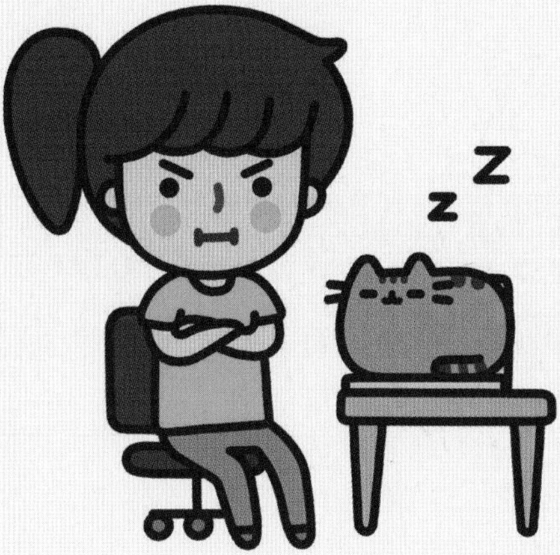
z Z

Yes

Pusheen's guide to being fancy

Not fancy

Kind of fancy?

Fancy

Super fancy

Fancy Pusheen

Pizza:
A how-to

1. Read recipe

2. Get ingredients

3. Preheat the oven

4. Make a huge mess
because you are a cat

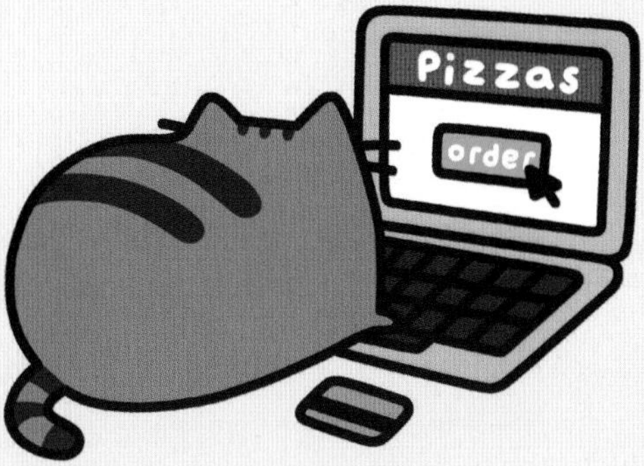
Pizzas
order

5. Order a pizza

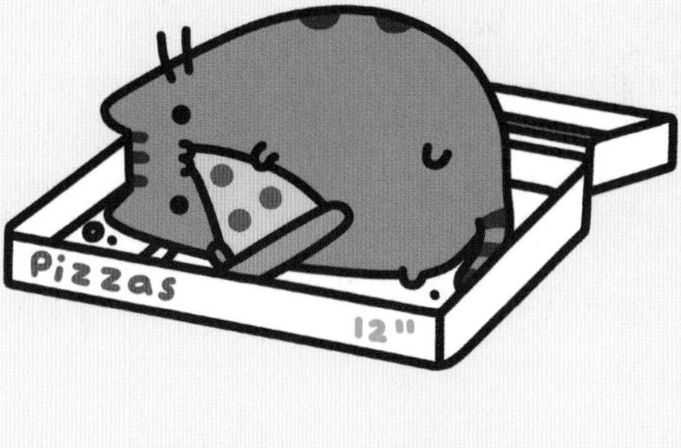
Pizzas
12"

6. Success!!!

With tiny paws

come tiny responsibilities

Cookies:
A how-to*

!!!

1. Want cookies

2. Choose a recipe

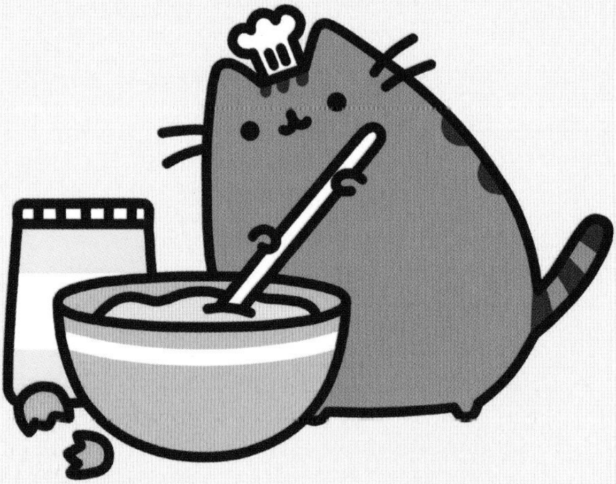

3. Mix the stuff

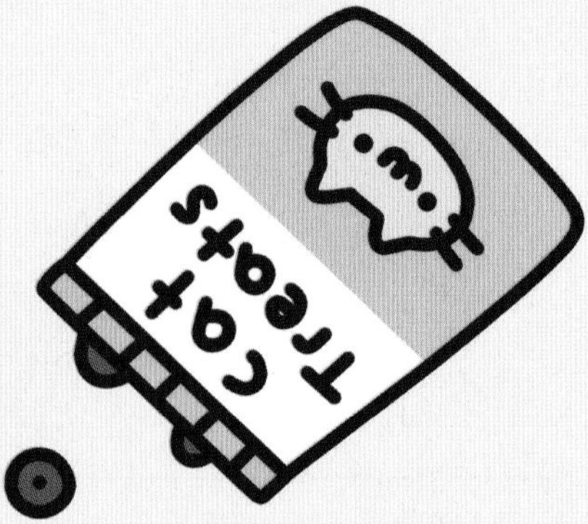
cat treats

4. Add candy

5. Taste the dough

6. All of it.

* Close enough

Big and

beautiful

Do-It-Yourself
Home Decor Tips
(from your cat)

DIY lace curtains

DIY chair cover

DIY shag rug

DIY floor lamp

How to have a great sleepover

1. Get makeovers

2. Watch scary movies

3. Eat junk food

4. Stay up all night

How to Procrastinate

Step 1: Ignore your work

Step 2: Have a snack

Step 3: Take a nap

Step 4: Forget what you were doing

Tech support tips

from your cat

Have you tried chewing on it?*

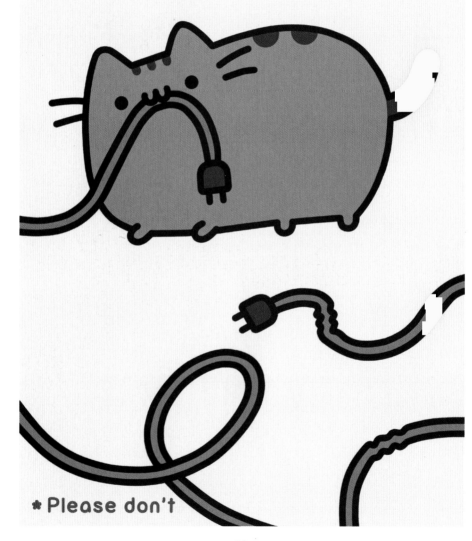

*Please don't

How about headbutting it?

Have you tried knocking it off of the desk?

How about staring at it?

Not helping?

Better sleep on it.

Pusheen's vacation to Japan

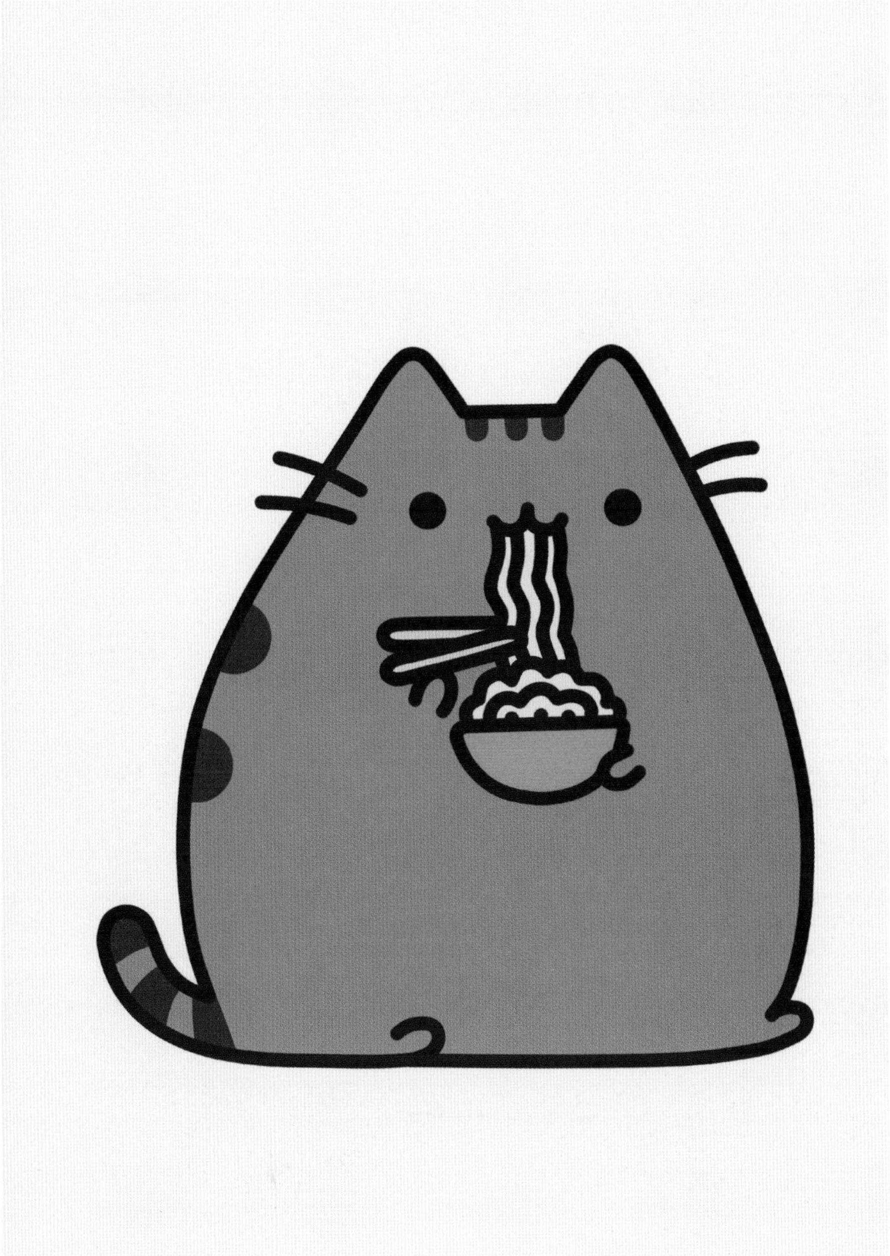

Part IV

Stormy

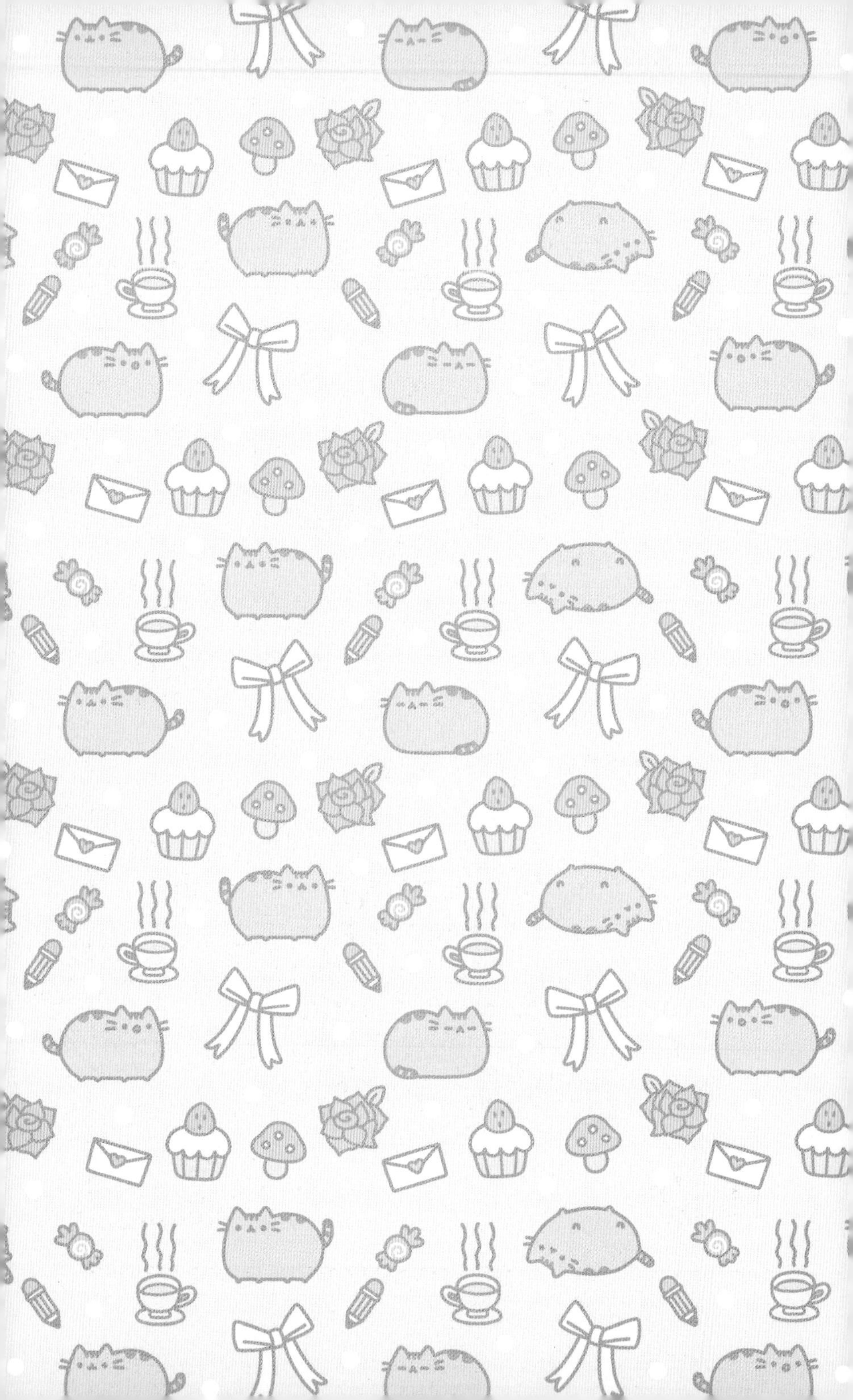

Name: Stormy
Birthday: Oct 24
Sex: Female
Best feature: My fluffy pants
Where I live: With my family
Hobbies: Chasing things
Favorite food: Kibbles & milk
Favorite word: "Wawa"
Dream: To grow up to be just
like my sister, Pusheen

The joys of having a younger sibling
(starring Stormy)

Mom says to share!

I'm telling.

Wasn't us.

Friends forever.

Kitten Adventures
with Stormy the Cat

The adventure

The reality

The adventure

The reality

The adventure

The reality

Stormy's guide to sleeping positions

The accordion

The storm cloud

The piggyback

Box size guide

The single

The double

The queen

The king

The princess

Cat Wizards

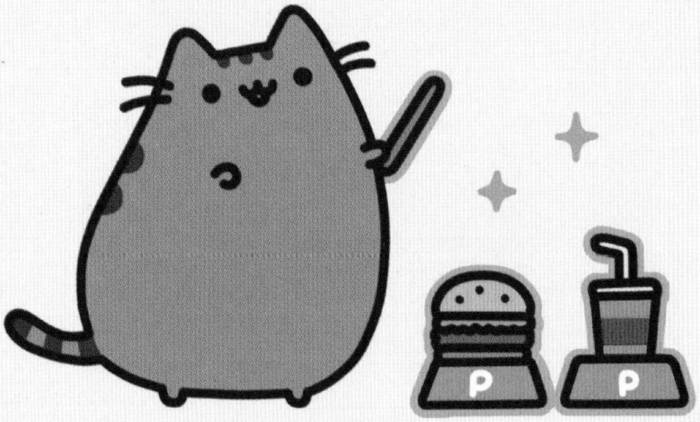
P
P

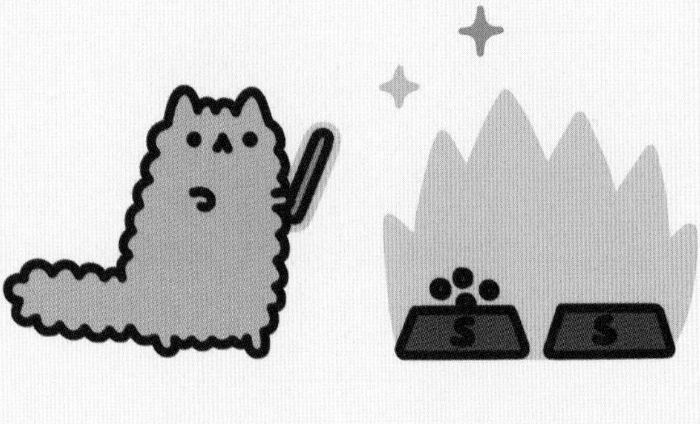
S
S

Which superpower would you choose?

1. Flight

2. Invisibility

3. Mind reading

4. Telekinesis

5. Super strength

6. Breathe underwater

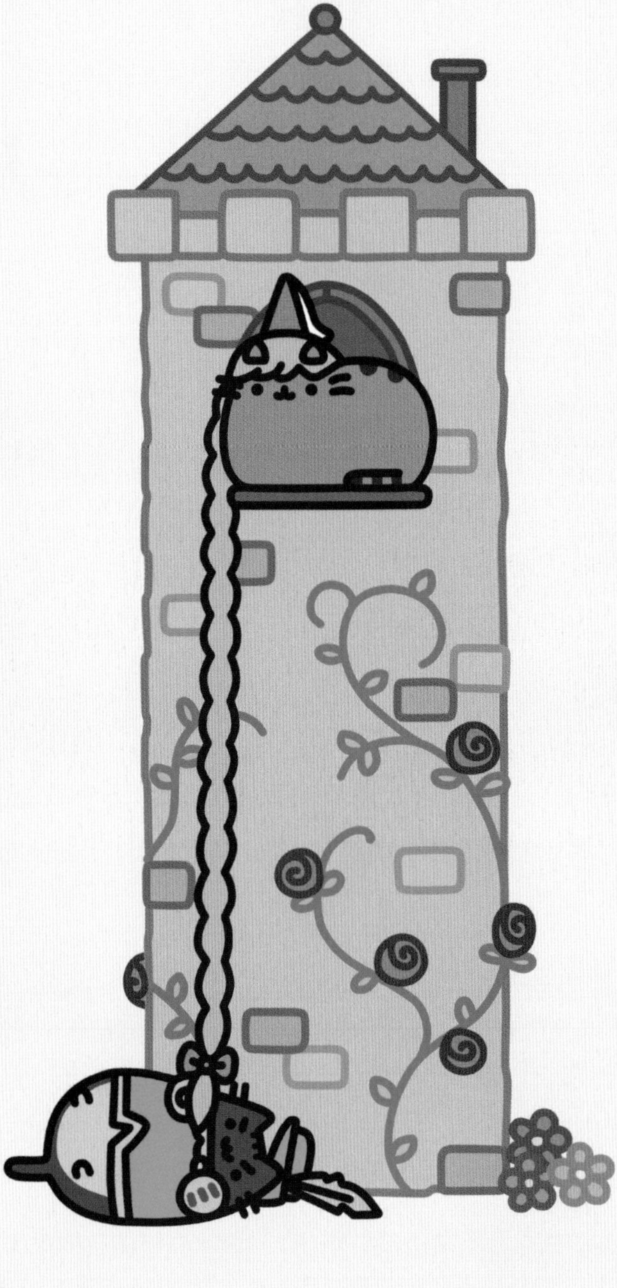

Part V

A Year in the Life of Pusheen

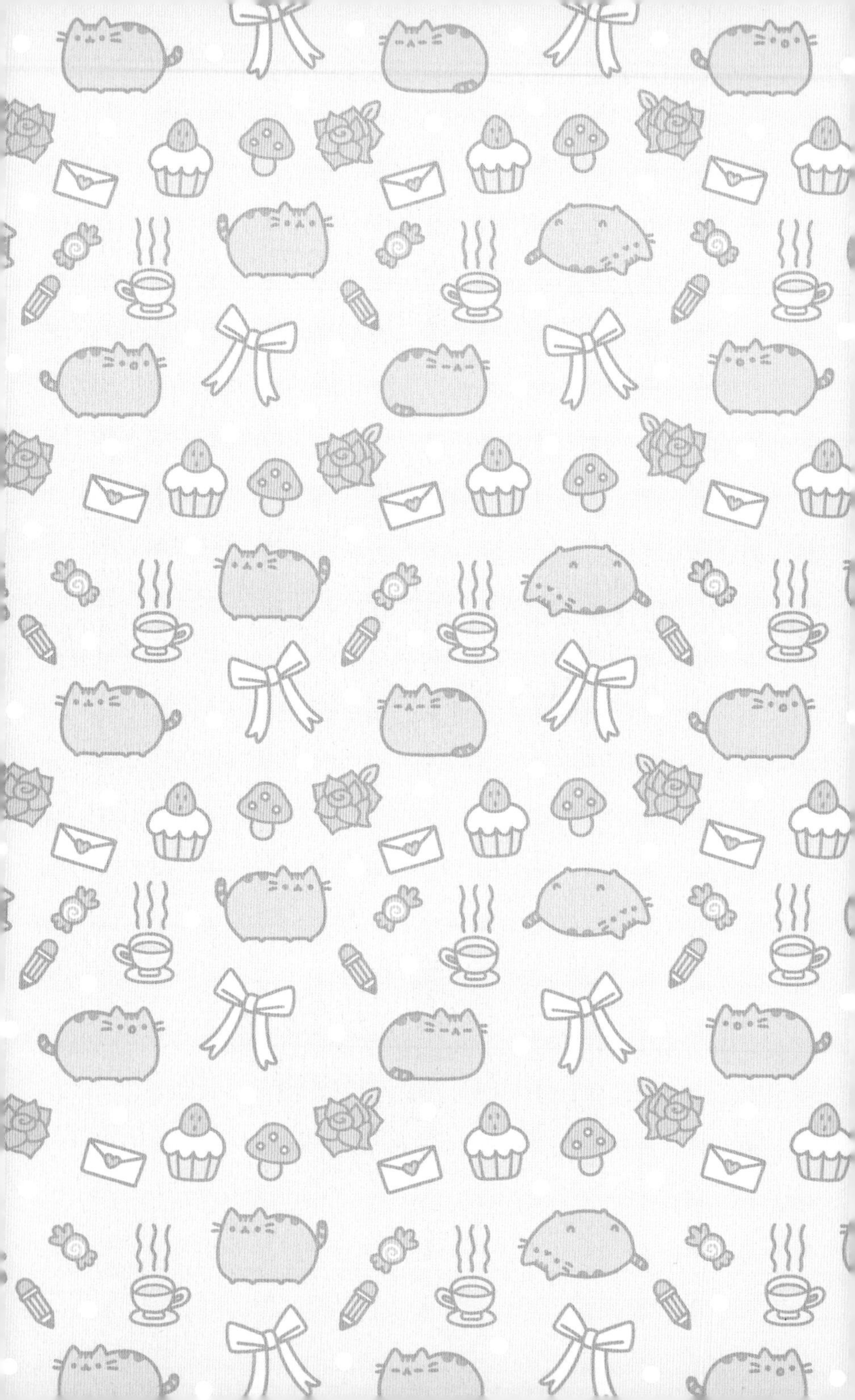

Three...

Two...

One...

HAPPY NEW YEAR!

New Year's resolutions

Expectation

Reality

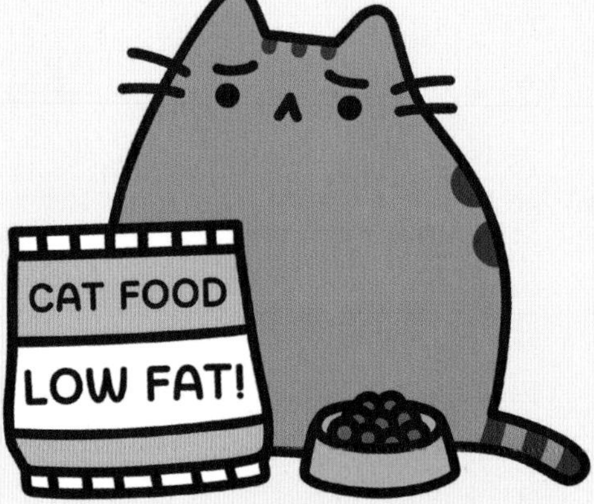
CAT FOOD
LOW FAT!

Expectation

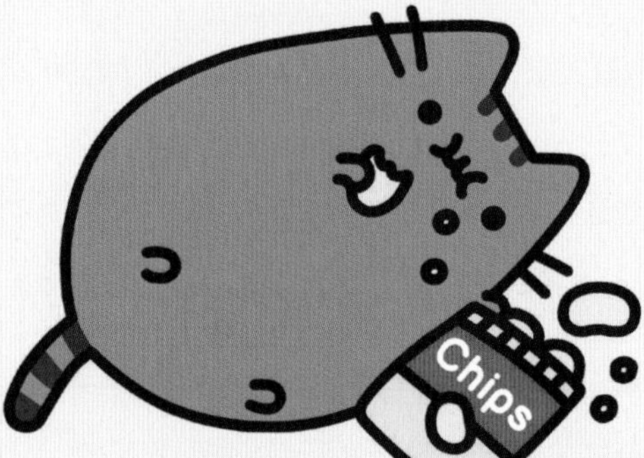
Chips

Reality

Valentines
from your cat

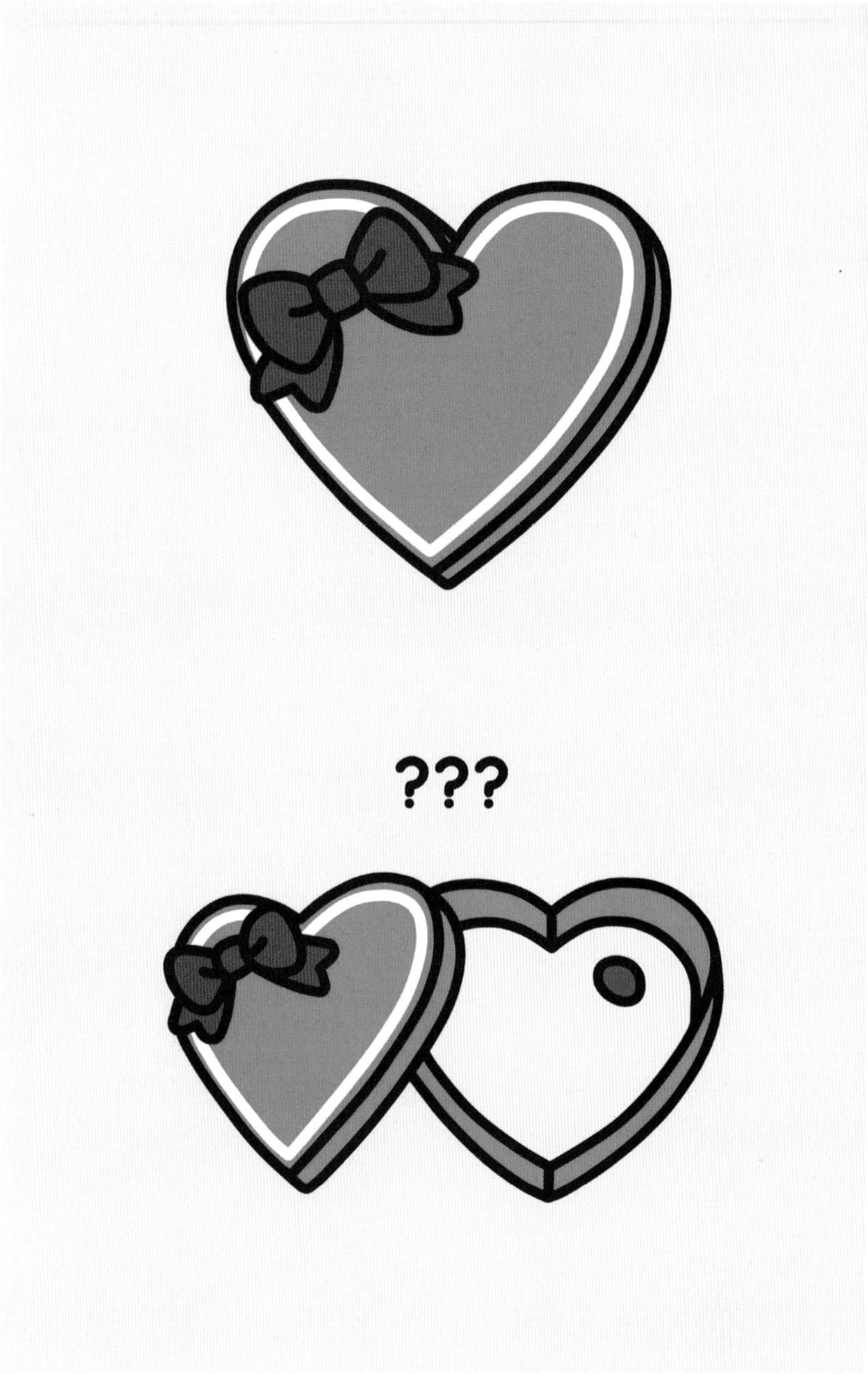
???

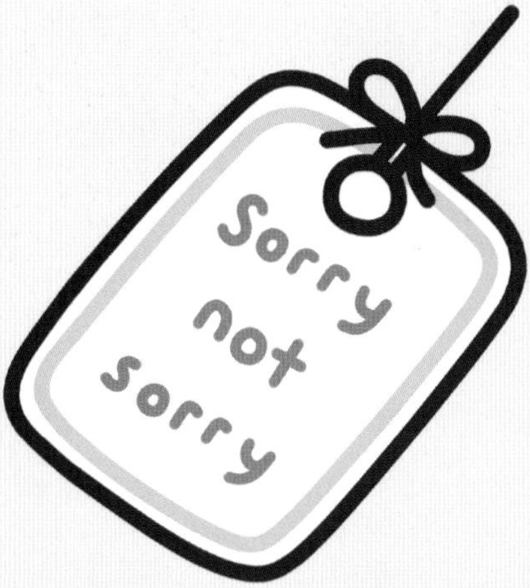
Sorry
not
sorry

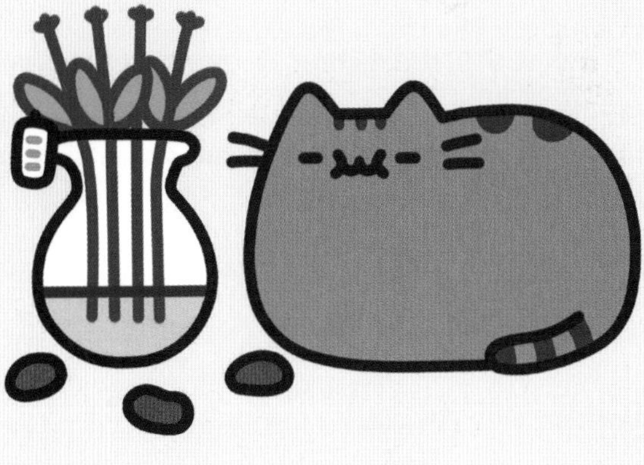

How to have a great Saint Patrick's Day

1. Have breakfast

2. Food coma

PET ME
I'M
IRISH

3. Wear green

Puisín (Pusheen) means "kitten"

4. Study Irish

5. Get lucky

Wake me up in spring

Reasons I love spring

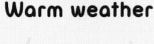

Warm weather

Easter

April showers

May flowers

Picnics

~~Bugs~~

Spring-cleaning guide

1. Clean the dishes

2. Clean out the fridge

3. Put away your toys

4. Prune the houseplants

5. Do the laundry

6. Dust everything

Summer

Expectation

Reality

Expectation

Reality

Expectation

Reality

How to celebrate on the
4ᵗʰ of July

1. Dress appropriately

2. Eat some BBQ

3. Think about eagles and stuff

4. Watch fireworks

My beach essentials

Donuts

Cake

Pizza

Bacon

Too hot.

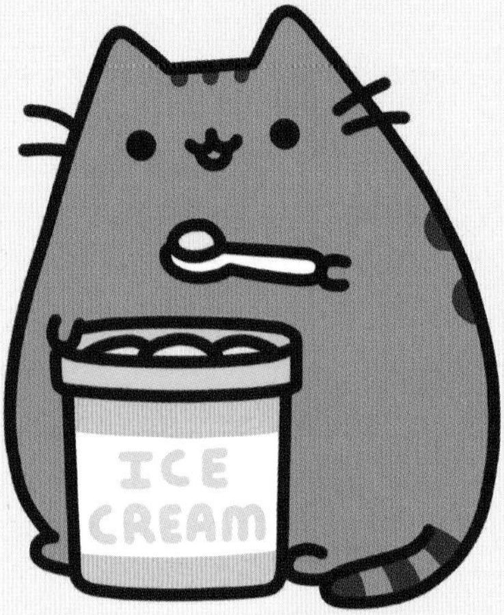
ICE
CREAM

Need ice cream.

Reasons I love fall

1. Pie

2. Pie

3. Pie

4. Pie

5. Pie

6. Also pie

BOO!

Lazy costume ideas
(for your cat)

A mummy

A ghost

A box

A witch

A superhero

A monster

No-shave November styling suggestions

The dad-stache

The scarf-stache

The Santa

The eyebrows

The elegante

~~The butt-stache~~
not recommended

How to Thanksgiving

The Pusheen way

1. Eat turkey

2. Eat pie

3. Eat turkey and pie

4. Take a nap

5. Wake up & repeat from step 1

5-second rule

How to make the best snowman

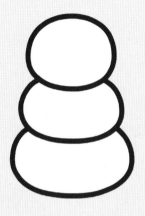

1. Make a body

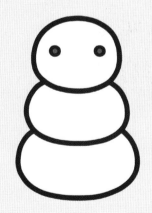

2. Add eyes

3. Add a smile

4. Add a nose

5. Add sprinkles

6. Enjoy!

Things your cat wants for
Christmas

✖ No

✔ Yes

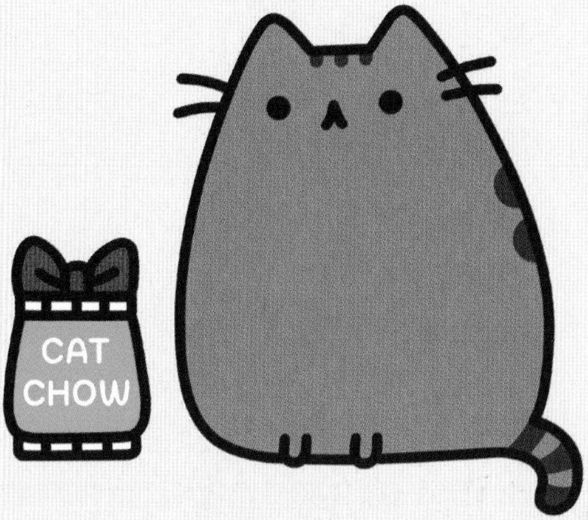
CAT
CHOW

✗ No

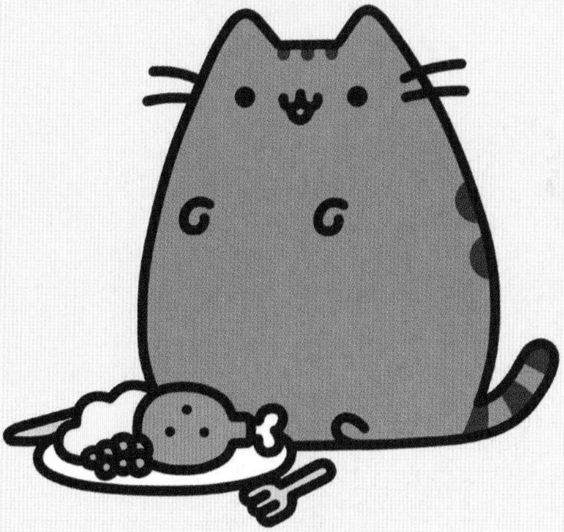

✓ Yes

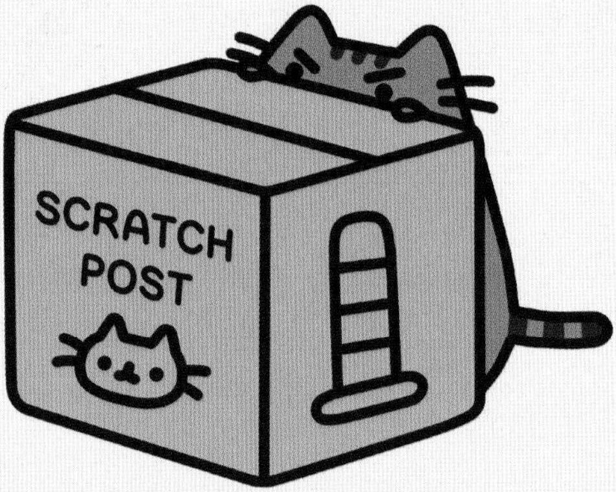
SCRATCH
POST

✗ No

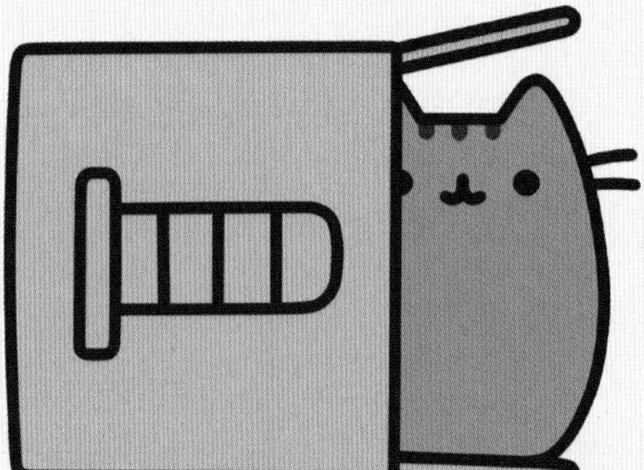

✓ Yes

Christmas

to-do list

☑ Decorate the tree

☑ Wrap the gifts

☑ Make cookies ~~for Santa~~

mrowrooomyao

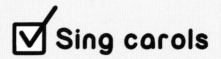
☑ Sing carols

☑ Spend time with family

DEC

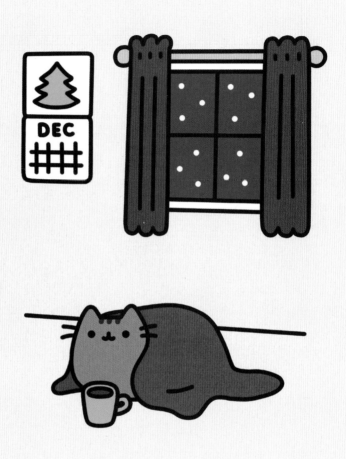

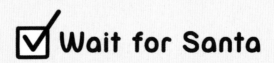

☑ Wait for Santa

How to catch Santa

1. Set your bait

2. Wait

3. Don't eat the bait

4. Don't do it

5. Stop!!

6. You ruined it

Have a Merry

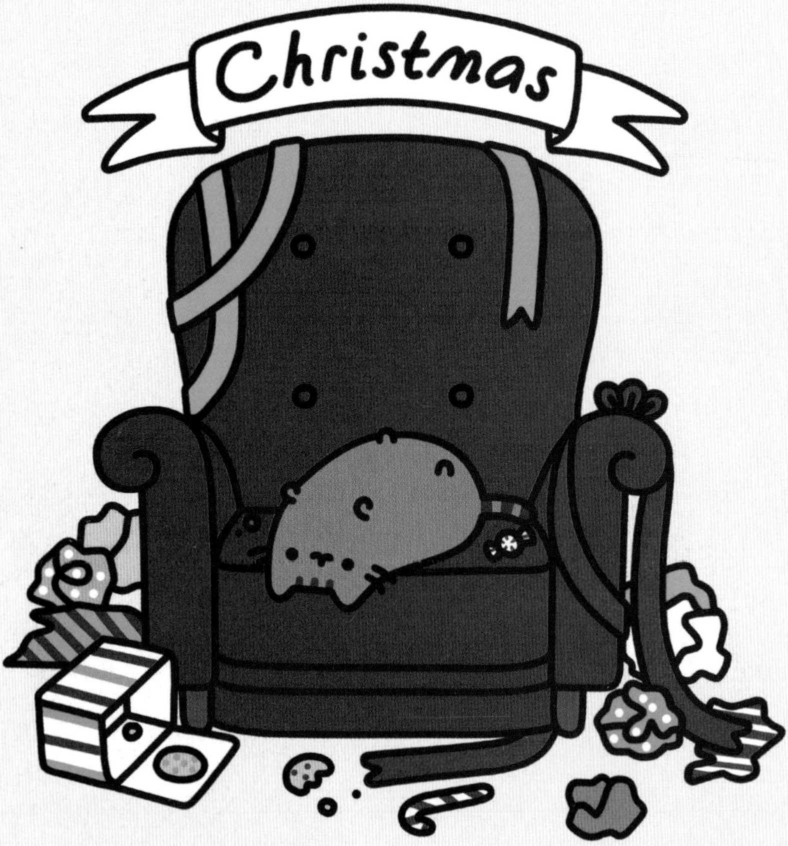
Christmas

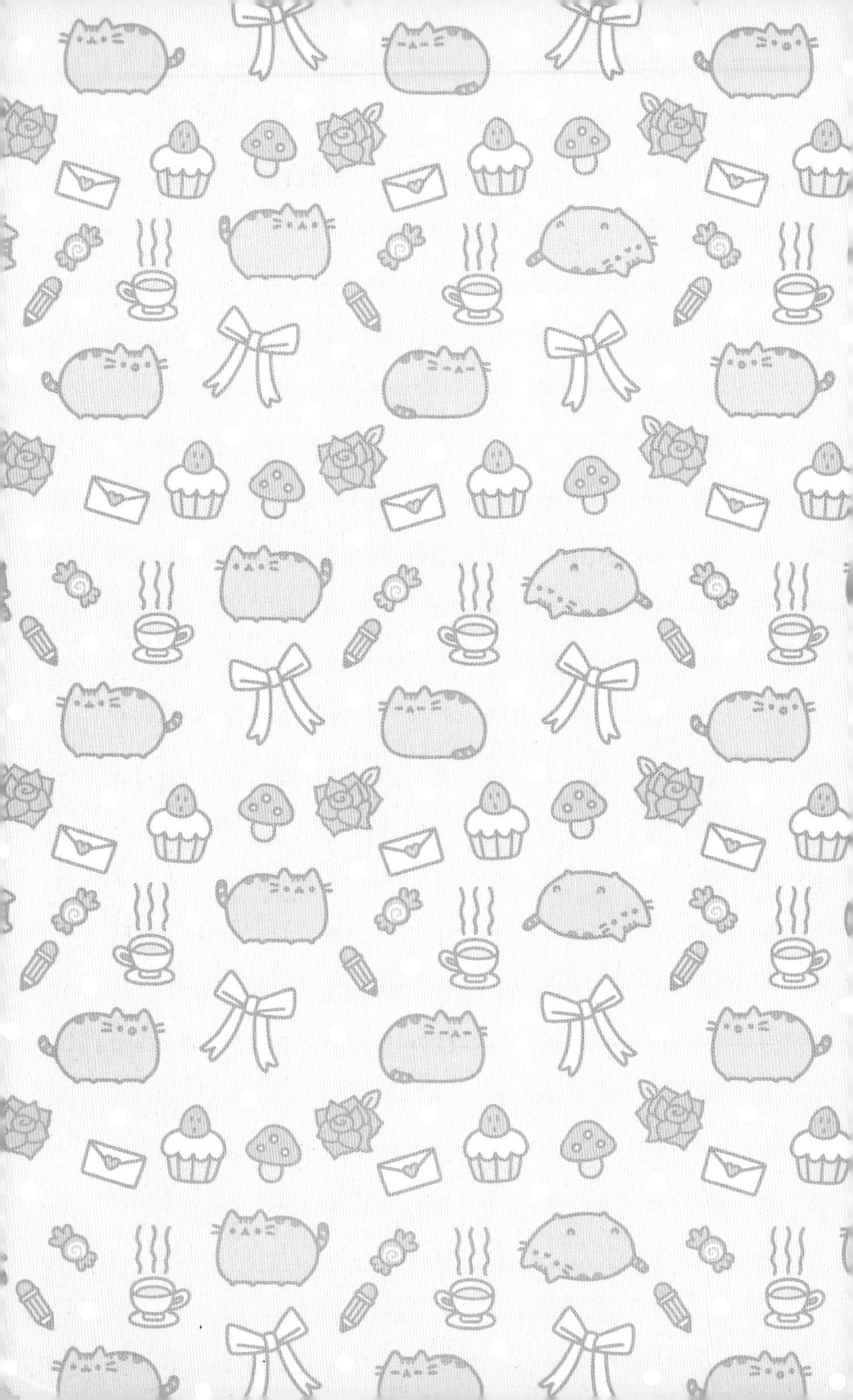

Acknowledgments

I would like to thank some of the amazing people in my life for all of the help and support they have given me throughout the process of creating this book.

Huge thanks go to my awesome literary agent, Myrsini Stephanides, who got this whole project rolling when she asked me if I'd ever consider making a Pusheen book. Without all of her help and guidance, this book wouldn't exist. Thank you, Myrsini!

I would also like to thank my fantastic editor, Michelle Howry, who has been an absolute delight to work with. She and her team at Touchstone have been so kind and enthusiastic about the project from day one, which really kept me motivated. I would especially like to thank Joy O'Meara for all of her hard work designing the interior of this book. You guys are the best.

To my family and friends, I honestly can't thank you all enough. Your love and support means the world to me. To my sister, Katie, thank you for your help with preparing my illustrations for print, and for all of those well-timed cups of tea. To my fiancé, Andrew, and his wonderful family, thank you for everything. Mom, Dad, Richard, Ryan, and Eve, thank you for always supporting me in whatever I choose to do, even when all I want to do is draw pictures of my cat.

A special thank-you to my good friends Hidehito Ikumo and Valerie Stern (LaylaLaneMusic.com) for your incredible support, and for always making sure I have great music to listen to while I work.

And most of all, thank you, Pusheen! You're one of my dearest friends, and I'm very lucky to be able to call myself your person. You're the best kitty and we all love you very much.

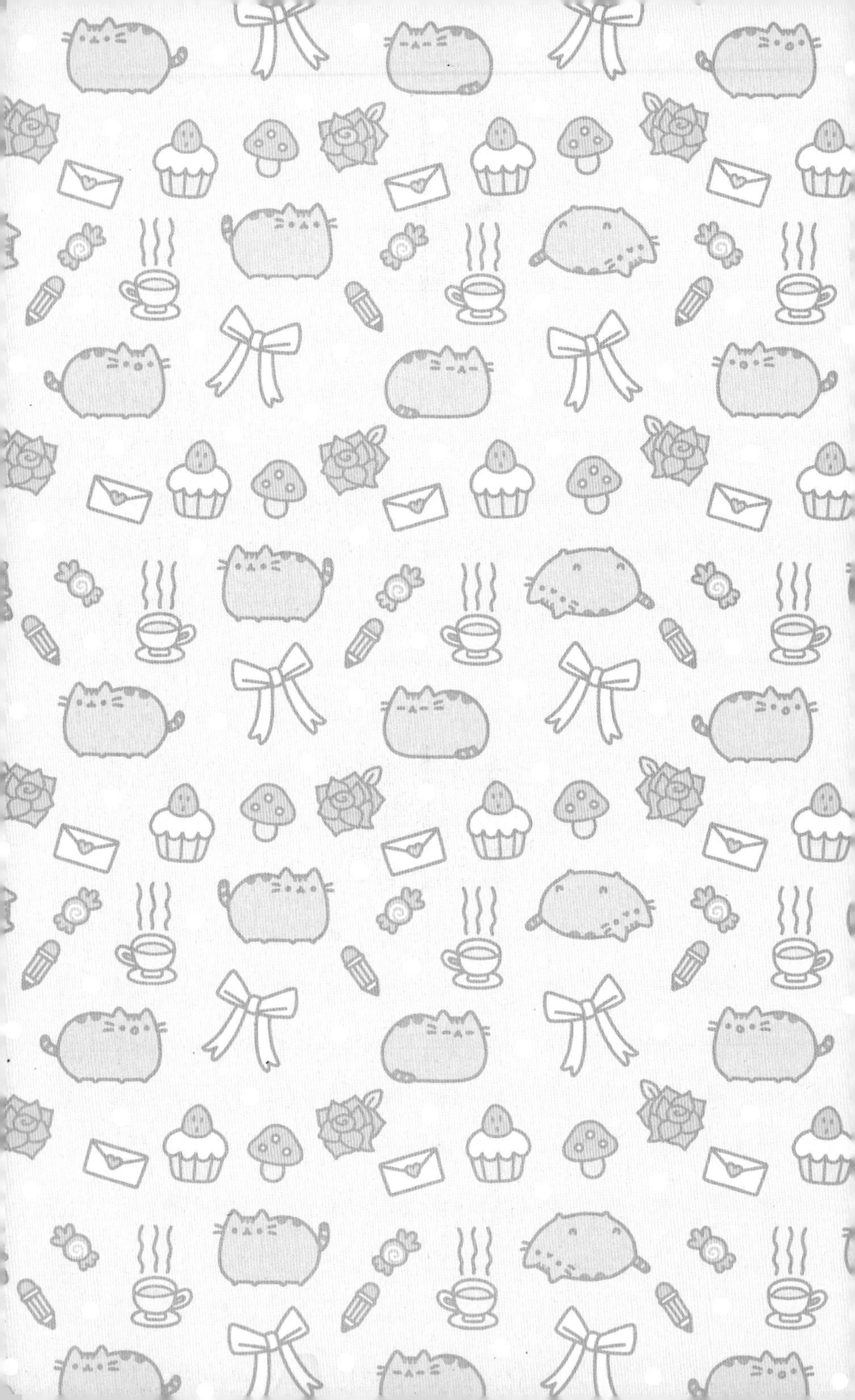

About the Author

Claire Belton is an artist currently living in the suburbs of Chicago with her fiancé, Andrew, and their cat, Stormy. Her hobbies include making art of all kinds, drinking tea, and traveling. Her past freelance work includes illustrations for clients such as Tokyopop, *Official U.S. PlayStation Magazine,* and Amaranth Games.

To see more of Claire's work, you can visit her art blog at Clairetonic.tumblr.com.

About Pusheen

Pusheen is a chubby gray tabby cat currently living in Connecticut with Claire's parents. She was adopted by Claire's family from an animal shelter in her youth and was named after the Irish word for kitten: *puisín.* Her hobbies include eating, sleeping, grooming herself, and generally being adorable.

To see more Pusheen, visit her website at Pusheen.com.

Home

is where my butt is.

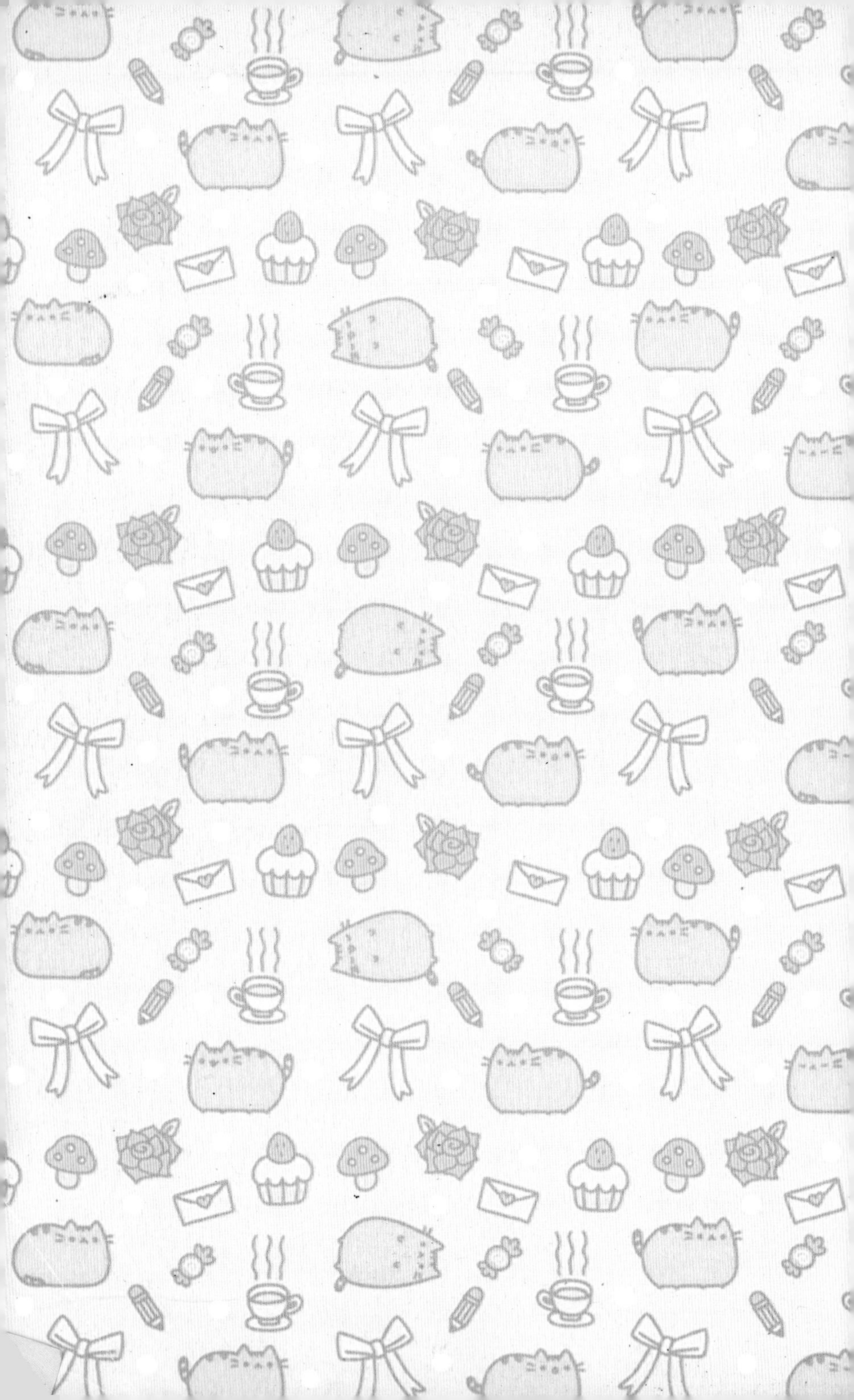